THE UNOFFICIAL OLiViA RODRIGO ACTIVITY BOOK

THE UNOFFICIAL OLIVIA RODRIGO ACTIVITY BOOK. Copyright © 2025 by Bluestone Books. All rights reserved. Any unauthorized duplication in whole or in part or dissemination of this edition by any means (including but not limited to photocopying, electronic devices, digital versions, and the internet) will be prosecuted to the fullest extent of the law.

Bluestone Books
www.bluestonebooks.co

ISBN: 978-1-965636-06-0 (trade paperback)

Printed in the United States of America
10 9 8 7 6 5 4 3 2 1

Cover illustration by Simone Douglas

Images used under license by Shutterstock.com

IMPORTANT NOTE TO READERS: This book has been written and published for entertainment purposes only. This book is independently authored and published and no sponsorship or endorsement of this book by, and no affiliation with Olivia Rodrigo or any trademarked brands or products mentioned within is claimed or suggested. All trademarks that appear in this book belong to their respective owners and are used here for informational purposes only. The author and publisher encourage readers to patronize Olivia Rodrigo's products and brands mentioned in this book.

THE UNOFFICIAL OLiViA ROdriGO ACTIVITY BOOK

TRIVIA, QUIZZES, GAMES, AND COLORING
— FOR —
FANS WITH GUTS

BLUESTONE BOOKS

CONTENTS

Introduction	6
Ballads of an All-American Songwriter	8
Influencing a Superstar Word Search	10
Girl's Got Guts	12
Olivia Affirmator	14
Perfect All-American	15
All About Olivia Crossword	16
Guitar Heroine Quiz	18
Liv's Leaked Songs Word Search	20
1 Step Forward, 3 Steps Back	22
Livie's Rad Sounds Crossword	24
Rodrigo Rhythms	26
Manifest Olivia Energy	28
The BFFs Word Search	30
The Butterfly Effect	32
Olivia's Favorite Things Crossword	34
Sour Scavenger Hunt	36
Wild Facts Quiz	38
Liv's Iconic Fashion Word Search	40

Butterfly Bingo 42
Behind the Music Crossword 44
Brutal Bracket 46
Butterfly Obsessed Quiz 48
In A Collab Word Search 50
This or That 52
True or False 53
Little-Known Liv Crossword 54
Songs of a *Sour* Sensation 56
A Songwriter at Heart 58
The Olivia Aesthetic Word Search 60
Olivia's Accolades 62
Girl She's Always Been Crossword 64
Livie Bingo 66
Causes to Care About Word Search 68
Get Him Back! 70
Songs of an Olivia Rodrigo Obsessive 72
Solutions 74

GO ALL IN ON OLIVIA

GOOD IDEA, RIGHT? The Unofficial Olivia Rodrigo Activity Book is the ultimate way to show off your Livie status. Flit like a butterfly across these purple pages to learn about Olivia's world, celebrate her music and lyrical prowess, channel her empowering attitude, and embrace the charm and sass from this songwriting sensation.

Maybe you have been following Olivia since her *Bizaardvark* days or her early guitar-strumming days on *High School Musical: The Musical: The Series*. Maybe you heard her hit the airwaves with her breakout single "drivers license," or you got really into her pop punk, vintage-loving style. No matter how you became "obsessed" with Olivia, you're here now, and you're about to embark on an activity book journey so fun you may just barf up glitter (just like your girl Liv).

Discover Olivia's roots with trivia about her musical inspirations, her favorite foods and family traditions, and the friends and boyfriends who have had a thing or two to do with her bold and confessional lyrics.

Find out how she's had an impact with "Girl's Got Guts" (page 12) and "The Butterfly Effect" (page 32). Summon her edgy attitude with the "Olivia Affirmator" (page 14) and "Manifest Olivia Energy" (page 28). Uncover more about the secrets of her music and songwriting with the "Guitar Heroine Quiz" (page 18), "Livie's Rad Sounds Crossword" (page 24), and the "In a Collab Word Search" (page 50).

As you bop around these pages, you'll find games to play with your Livies like "Butterfly Bingo" (page 42) and "1 Step Forward, 3 Steps Back" (page 22). But if you're feeling like some quiet time is "good 4 u," you'll find coloring pages that get in on Olivia's vibe and tracker pages where you can write down your favorite songs and lyrics and what they mean to you.

Turn up your Olivia playlist or put the needle on her records as you dive into this all-Olivia, all-the-time activity book. Get the inside scoop on your favorite pop star with a "riot grrrl" attitude, then relax with games and coloring pages that will certify your Olivia Rodrigo superfan status!

BALLADS OF AN ALL-AMERICAN SONGWRITER

Olivia's got range. Whether it's her punk-inspired bangers or soft, hushed poetics, Olivia's music has a little something for everyone. Below, you can find anagrams of some of her song titles. Use the clues to help you unscramble these hits.

1. During her *Tiny Desk Concert*, Olivia explained that the first version of this song came from a homework assignment at her University of Southern California poetry class.

    YCAL

2. Hayley Williams and Josh Farro received writing credits for this Olivia Rodrigo song that shares similarities with their 2007 Paramore hit "Misery Business."

    DOGO 4 U

3. This song appeared on the soundtrack of *The Hunger Games: The Ballad of Songbirds & Snakes*.

    NATC' CCHTA EM ONW

4. The opening line of this song, "I am light as a feather and as stiff as a board" recalls a childhood séance game.

    LAL-CRIMENAA *BHCT

5. This chart-topper was Olivia's first single off her debut album *SOUR* and transformed her from a likable Disney actress to a superstar overnight.

    IRSDREV NESLCIE

6. Olivia gave interpolation credits to Taylor Swift and Jack Antonoff for this song.

   1 ESTP WOFRRAD 3 TSSPE KCAB

7. Olivia had a couple of relationships with significant age gaps when she was 18 and 19. Fans speculate that this song was written about one or (or both!) of her older exes.

   IPAVEMR

8. Olivia's songs have creative introductions. This second single off *GUTS* starts with the creaking of an opening door.

   ADB EDIA ?HTGRI

9. This song uses wordplay to humorously describe wanting to get revenge on and also reunite with a toxic ex.

   TGE IMH !KACB

10. This emotional and compassionate song has Olivia extending love and support to friends who were mistreated by their families.

    EPHO RU KO

INFLUENCING A SUPERSTAR WORD SEARCH

It's no secret that Olivia got her early music taste from her parents, who raised her on Pearl Jam, No Doubt, and The White Stripes. But this sour prom princess gives credit to many other musicians. See if you can find them in the word search.

```
E N I H C A M E H T T S N I A G A E G A R
D K A C E Y M U S G R A V E S L W B L M J
N N Z T J J V G B Y R B L Y A W P M K B L
A O W Y A L D M J B Y P N N M D J B G M K
L T N J Q Y J L L L P L I D B N D D K Y K
Y S P Y T T L C N A G S N Y R Q V W D D
O E R X Q Y A O A B M X D D W M L B L J L
T L W D L R P N R O I N A F E T S N E W G
N D Q N D B O B R S Y G Z X N M L N J N
I D N I Y I D I M L W D P E R Z Q P D Z L
S I B Y F M S N J P D I C P Q B V Q P Y B
E H B G Z S Y M R P T N F Z N Z Z R D Z B
B M N T E T Z K X D I J M T Z R Y R Z X Y
A O N T L J V B W V W B B B B P R L N M M Y
B T T K T Z Q T T T T R M Y N M G B V W Y
M E M T Z X D S R R Q Y D D T P Y Y R M V
E M B D P D N Q T D R Z Q K Z R N D Z V D
```

TAYLOR SWIFT
RAGE AGAINST THE MACHINE
ALANIS MORISSETTE
ST. VINCENT
BABES IN TOYLAND

CARDI B
GWEN STEFANI
TOM HIDDLESTON
FIONA APPLE
KACEY MUSGRAVES

GIRL'S GOT GUTS

SHOWING UP.
Olivia acted as the bridge between the Biden-Harris administration and Gen-Z during the rollout of the very first Covid-19 vaccines to battle the 2020 pandemic. On July 13, 2021, she graced the White House and met with President Biden, Vice President Harris, and Chief Medical Advisor Anthony Fauci to answer questions about the vaccines for social media audiences. Donning the "Dark Brandon" shades alongside President Biden in her pink Chanel suit, Olivia played a huge role in spreading vaccine awareness.

SAY IT LOUDER FOR THE PEOPLE IN THE BACK.
Olivia refers to her 2023 appearance at the Glastonbury Festival as her favorite performance. She used her voice to speak up for women's rights on stage, teaming up with popular British singer Lily Allen in an energetic, upbeat performance. The two stole the show as they sang a duet of Allen's most popular song.

NO

CHARITY MATTERS.

Olivia is a vocal advocate and philanthropist for the treatment and cure of epidermolysis bullosa, a rare condition that causes blistering skin. On November 18, 2021, she donated an autographed Gibson guitar to the #VentureIntoCures fundraiser. She and other celebs helped raise $6 million for the cause.

CHECKING HER RESOURCES.

Olivia gained attention during her *GUTS* world tour in 2024 by providing women's health resources and voter registration booths at many of her shows.

OLIVIA SUPPORTS WOMEN.

Portions of her *SOUR* ticket sales were donated in support of Women for Women International, which helps women who have survived war and conflict situations to rebuild their lives. In October 2023, Olivia launched Fund 4 Good, which supports women's reproductive healthcare. And across her *GUTS* world tour, she donated a portion of concert ticket proceeds to various organizations, including more than 600 women's shelters in Canada and a program called Women Against Violence Europe.

OLIVIA AFFIRMATOR

Olivia's got attitude, and she uses it to acknowledge feelings and inspire confidence. Decorate this page with your favorite wisdom from Olivia's songs or something you have heard her say in an interview. Treat this like your personal slogan and make it stand out with big letters, bright colors, and even glitter. Use this as your reminder to walk the walk like Olivia does.

PERFECT ALL-AMERICAN

Olivia's lyrics are known for being confessional, raw, and edgy. She pushes back on societal standards of perfection by emphatically singing that "pretty isn't pretty," suggesting that there's always more to someone than what the eye can see. Charlie Gunn of The Forty-Five called *SOUR* "the greatest coming-of-age album since early Taylor Swift or Lorde" for these very reasons. Check out the word cloud below to think about some of the things that make Olivia so magnetic, and then write your thoughts about what words jump out to you the most.

ALL ABOUT OLIVIA CROSSWORD

Discover some of the most interesting facts about Olivia's life and her upbringing.

ACROSS
2. Her favorite road trip destination.
5. The affectionate name used for Olivia Rodrigo fans.
6. The first concert Olivia attended.
8. Olivia's favorite color.
9. Her middle name.

DOWN
1. Olivia's heritage is German through her mom and this through her dad.
3. The name of Olivia's hometown in California.
4. Olivia's star sign.
7. The number of siblings Olivia has.

GUITAR HEROINE QUIZ

A pianist at heart, Olivia has said that playing guitar doesn't come naturally to her. She's said that "it's nice to go out of your comfort zone" and that she works hard to learn how to use picks when she's more comfortable strumming with her fingers. Take this quiz to test your knowledge on Olivia's guitar chops or learn as you go:

1. Olivia learned to play guitar by strumming pop songs in her bedroom, but not without a push. Her character in this show needed to know how to play guitar, so Olivia did too.

   _____

2. In which of Olivia's ballads does she use a rubber bridge? A rubber bridge is a piece of rubber that sits against the strings of a guitar to give it a softer, deeper sound than the guitar would play without it.

   _____

> The purple bowtie-shaped guitar from "obsessed" was custom-made for Olivia, but the guitar itself was designed by cowriter of the song and music icon, St. Vincent. The "Goldie" guitar is special for its female-friendly design. Few guitars are designed by women, and this one has a smaller, lighter frame, making it easier on the shoulders.

3. At the beginning of the *GUTS* tour in April 2023, Olivia played this "secret" song—which would end up on the *GUTS* (*spilled*) album—with an Ernie Ball Music Man St. Vincent Goldie guitar.

   _____

4. Olivia frequently plays a Gibson L-00, and she even had a giveaway with a signed version on her website. She gave it away in this color.

   _____

LIV'S LEAKED SONGS WORD SEARCH

A singer-songwriter by craft, Olivia takes a leaf from Taylor Swift's book, having written far more songs than ever made it to the airwaves. Here are ten of her unreleased songs that were originally recorded for *SOUR* or *GUTS* but were ultimately cut from the albums.

```
S B T E A S T R O N A U T M D
E T D I V G T D Y S A T N A F
Z F R J U O V X X D L J R K S
T X I A M Q L K G B J W T O W
M Z X L N R I I N B R D B J Y
Q G R N R G E M S J D E V D W
J T M Y B O E T O E R Y S J M
B N B G R G F R T M N T N N L
Y T B D R R Q N S E R O W R W
T V G R P Y Q P O A B J E J K
N Y L M J R J T N S G O L H J
N M R Z D L N G B G I A D N T
J M T Z P R E R B B L R I T M
T L G J X M R M M D N V P N N
```

ASTRONAUT
DO BETTER
FANTASY

MOM I QUIT
PRISON FOR LIFE
SOBER

STRANGE
STRANGERS AGAIN
THE ONES I LOVE

1 STEP FORWARD, 3 STEPS BACK

Agree to disagree with your fellow Livies. To play this game inspired by the song off of Olivia's debut album *SOUR*, grab a friend or two and a single die, then roll for your turn. If you land on a space that has a 👄 and the statement is true for you, **take 3 steps back**. If the space has a 🦋 and the statement is true for you, **take 1 step forward to the next clue**.

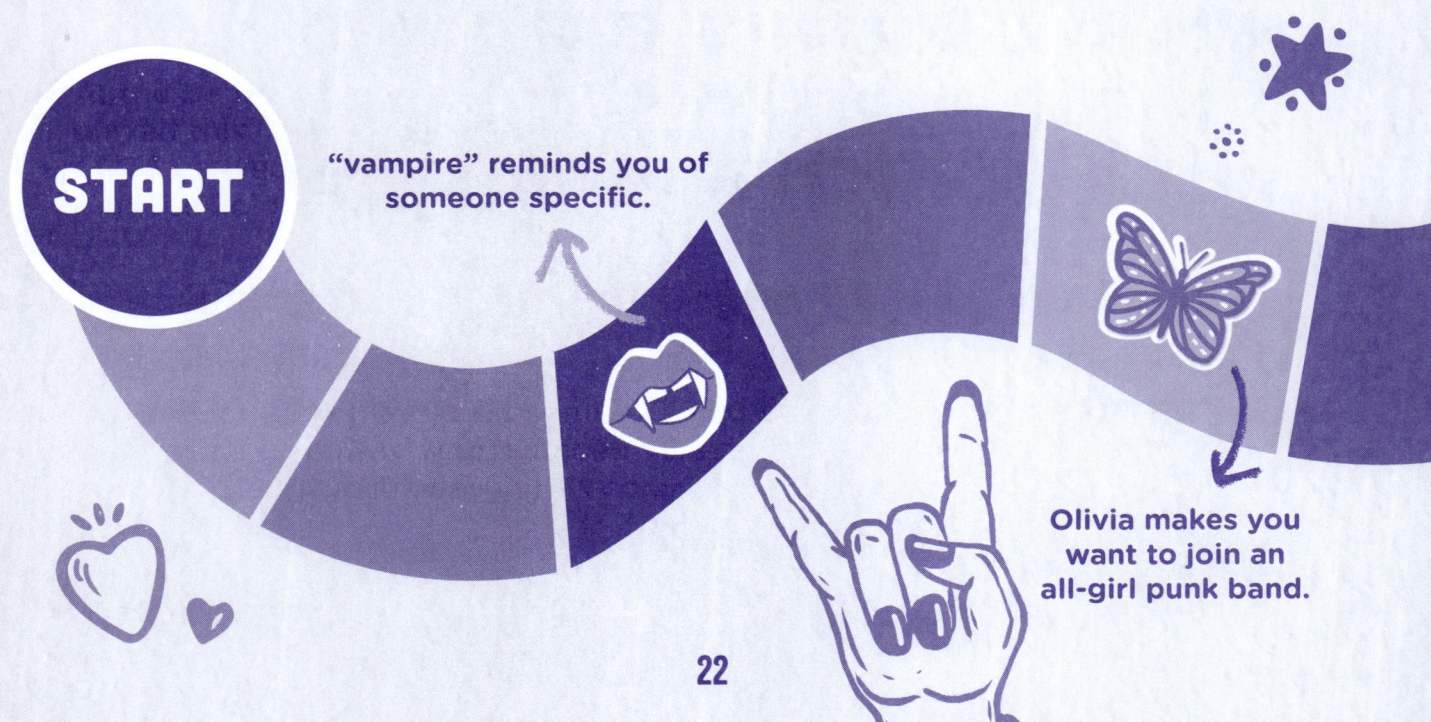

- "vampire" reminds you of someone specific.
- Olivia makes you want to join an all-girl punk band.

LIVIE'S RAD SOUNDS CROSSWORD

Many of Olivia's tracks use everyday sounds and ambient noise to create a relatable energy. Find out some of her most interesting techniques here.

ACROSS

3 The beginning of this song features the tinny, melodic tones of a glockenspiel.
4 The sound of a car door chime plays alongside the beat in this song.
5 A moog synthesizer, invented in 1964 by Robert Moog, is used in this hit song.
6 The sound of an amp adjusting is the first sound you hear in "ballad of a homeschooled _____."

DOWN

1 "1 step forward, 3 steps back" takes sonic cues from "New Year's Day" by this artist and includes her favorite number in the title.
2 That's no instrument. This chorus features Olivia's shriek, which gradually increases in intensity.

RODRIGO RHYTHMS

There's no end to Olivia's creativity, from pushing the limits in her music videos to genre-bending in her sounds. Below, you can find anagrams of some of her song titles. Use the clues to help you unscramble these hits.

1. The music video for this song features Olivia standing on top of cars in traffic surrounded by ballerinas in tutus.
   ULRTAB

2. Olivia credits scrolling "breakup TikTok" and seeing a hopeful video as the inspiration for this song.
   GHNEUO RFO OUY

3. The premise of the music video for this song was based on a Reddit post that said, "If all your exes were in one room together, what would be the outcome?"
   EDESBOSS

4. Olivia's producer Dan Nigro discovered her music from her social media post of this song, which she'd thought about deleting.
   REIAPPH

5. Olivia had wanted to scrap this song from her album, and it ended up being #3 on the Billboard Hot 100.
   JDAE UV

6. Nominated for "Best Rock Song" at the 66th Annual Grammys, this song lost out to "Not Strong Enough" by boygenius.

   ALALDB FO A OLEDOEOMHHSC LIGR

7. Fans speculated that the thirteen-second intro and thirteen-second outro of this song hints at a feud between Olivia and Taylor Swift—a theory Olivia has refuted.

   HET GDGRUE

8. Olivia wrote this song in her living room after a night of overthinking and replaying embarrassing moments in her head.

   EVOL SI RSARSAMEBGNI

9. Olivia uses this song to highlight the emotional toll of unrealistic beauty standards.

   TPTYRE TSNI' ERTYTP

10. A departure from her punk and rock sounds in other songs, this track takes its cues from country music.

    LRIG 'VEI WYAALS ENEB

MANIFEST OLIVIA ENERGY

Olivia has a gift that many artists don't: in addition to being extremely talented and hardworking, she's authentic. She's not afraid to mess up, and part of her charm is that she bares her messy emotions for everyone to see. This gives her fans an eye into her world, but it also makes her music all the more relatable. In an interview, she said, "As I get older, I realize that, if I were only to make things that were perfect, I would literally never make anything at all." With her albums *SOUR* and *GUTS*, Olivia shows that courage is sometimes found in embracing the imperfect side of things. Inside the letters below, write out all of the imperfect qualities that make you unique and special, or the ones that you admire in Olivia herself.

THE BFFs WORD SEARCH

Liv's got no shortage of admirers, and she's always warned us about "fair-weather friends." But it's the friends she's gathered along the way—from growing up on the Disney Channel together to meeting after she'd launched into superstardom—who matter most. In the word search, see if you can find some of Liv's favs.

```
R K L J M T D V D X A Y Y T
R E L G E I Z E I D D A M C
Z W W Z K N T D D X G W H N
L P O Y R J N I Y G D A Y M
Y Y J T B L S A G Q R W Y R
U V A M A O L E O L Q W N E
H P N R N P R A I R B V A G
N N R R G G A D U Q T R R G
O R A N I N A S R F C E J G
S E V N J M A P I M E R G V
I T A J E Y M N E R X Y P A
D V G L N N R T O D I V Y T
A D I T R M A Q Y C K Y R V
M O L J D T B Z W Y B D Y W
```

JENNA ORTEGA **MADDIE ZIEGLER**
MADISON HU **CHARLI D'AMELIO**
TATE MCRAE **ADDISON RAE**
CONAN GRAY **LAUFEY**
IRIS APATOW **AVANI GREGG**

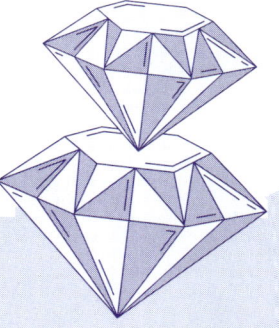

THE BUTTERFLY EFFECT

Olivia embraces positive energy, creativity, and liberation in her music. Her "riot grrrl" attitude, reminiscent of female punk acts of the 1990s, gives her songs a mix of attitude, mischief, empowerment, and playfulness that's both inspiring and fun to listen to. In the butterflies here, you'll see some moments when Olivia was transformational. In the blank butterflies, fill in your favorite inspirations—whether they're something Olivia did or something that happened in your own life.

Olivia's band is made up entirely of women and nonbinary musicians.

At her *GUTS* show in Manila, Olivia donated her ticket sales to Jhpiego, a healthcare nonprofit for women and girls in the Philippines. The show was her biggest yet with 55,000 fans, showing just how generous this gesture truly was.

In October 2021, Olivia became the first musician to record a full-length set at Austin City Limits with an all-female band.

OLIVIA'S FAVORITE THINGS CROSSWORD

Discover some of the most interesting facts about Olivia's life and her upbringing.

ACROSS

1. She can't leave the house without these.
5. She's been writing in this since she was thirteen.
7. Olivia's favorite coffee shop order. Hint: it's iced.
8. A self-described germaphobe, Olivia always brings her own one of these to a hotel.

DOWN

2. She snacks on this treat all day, especially at her piano.
3. Her morning ritual is just like this, but for *The New York Times*.
4. A fan once gave her one of these depicting the Eiffel Tower, which she uses every day.
6. Olivia is a big fan of craft soda made famous by this state.

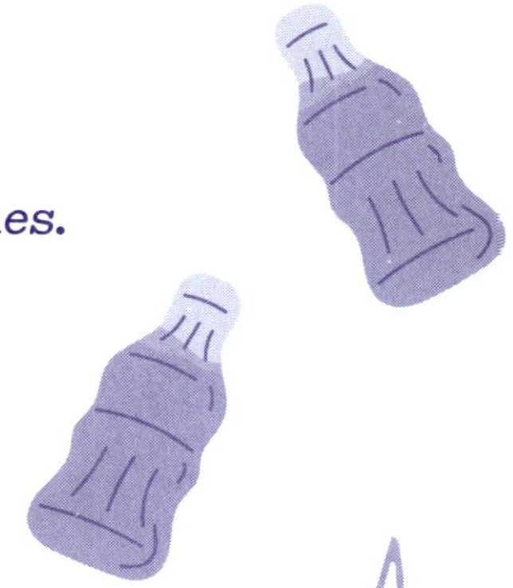

SOUR SCAVENGER HUNT

Using an instant camera or your social stories, take photos and videos of yourself going full Olivia with each of these tasks. Make a game out of it with friends and see who completes each of the tasks first!

STANDING IN A "SOUR PROM" POSE WITH A FRIEND

WEARING BUTTERFLY WINGS, HAIRCLIPS, OR ACCESSORIES

COVERING YOUR FACE WITH STICKERS

MAKING GLITTER YOUR WHOLE PERSONALITY

PLAYING THE PIANO

DRESSING UP LIKE OLIVIA

PRETENDING TO THROW UP GLITTER

LISTENING TO OLIVIA'S MUSIC

DROPPING A TROPHY

POSING WITH HER RECORD

POWER CLASHING

HOLDING A MEGAPHONE

BAKING STAR OR HEART COOKIES

WEARING FANGS

PLAYING THE GUITAR

Olivia won three Grammys in 2022 for Best New Artist, Best Pop Vocal Album, and Best Pop Solo Performance for her song, "drivers license." When she was posing for a photo with her armful of trophies, she accidentally dropped one and it broke in half.

WILD FACTS QUIZ

Livie knows how to rock an animal print, but these facts are even wilder.
See if you can stump your friends with these little-known Rodrigo secrets.

1. This song off *SOUR* claims an unusual statistic: it has the most listens of any song that is the *least-listened-to* song on any album on Spotify.

   _____

2. Olivia has "baby synesthesia," which is a rare neurological condition that lets her do what when she hears music?

   _____

3. Which famous singer sang background vocals for both *SOUR* and *GUTS*?

   _____

4. Olivia released the song "vampire" thirteen years to the day after the release of this blockbuster.

   _____

LIV'S ICONIC FASHION WORD SEARCH

Punk, sweet, and sour, Olivia Rodrigo manages to be all things at once. Her unapologetic attitude gives her the driver's license to wear whatever she wants, whether it's a punk-rock schoolgirl outfit or her very best power-clashing fits, like the leopard-print handbag and polka dot halter she wore in a photo shoot on a New York City subway car. Find these fashion phrases in the word search.

Olivia loves vintage and knows how to use it. When she visited the White House in the summer of 2021 to support Covid-19 vaccination efforts, Olivia and her stylist Chenelle Delgadillo made sure her attire was demure but informed. She donned a 1995 vintage Karl Lagerfeld Chanel suit in pink, which offered subtle nods to women before her. From *Clueless*'s Cher Horowitz and *Legally Blonde*'s Elle Woods to First Lady Jacqueline Kennedy Onassis, iconic women have made a cultural impact wearing just such a suit.

```
P Y T T Z L R J T P E Q Z V X
D A L Q J B X N Q N C Y P M Q
P R T L D N Q R X J A G P Q R
O K S T O O B K C A L B P Y X
L D R D E T R I K S I N I M K
K G R M A R Y J A N E S P N J
A S M A P J N Z N Z V Y U B J
D Y N G P X Q E X W B P D L R
O T Y E X O N W D W B T B E J
T V L Z A D E G R T L B D N Z
J K Z P G K B L V T I L M V Q
D Y R G M Q E Z D L I G D L Q
J T W N B G Y R K P W K H K L
Q N N L J L D R S Y R X Y T J
X Y B Q L X J Y T P Y L N N S
```

MINI SKIRT
BLACK BOOTS
PATTERNED TIGHTS
MARY JANES
RED LIPS

LEOPARD
POLKA DOT
SNEAKERS
LACE
PUNK

BUTTERFLY BINGO

Turn up your Olivia radio, hit shuffle, and play bingo in teams of two. When you hear a song that's on your board, put a piece of candy or a sticker on that spot. Whoever gets five in a row first wins.

"GOOD 4 U!"	"ALL-AMERICAN B*TCH"	"OBSESSED"	"TRAITOR"	"DEJA VU"
"DRIVERS LICENSE"	"LACY"	"VAMPIRE"	"LOGICAL"	"THE GRUDGE"
"BALLAD OF A HOME-SCHOOLED GIRL"	"SCARED OF MY GUITAR"	FREE	"GET HIM BACK!"	"MAKING THE BED"
"LOVE IS EMBARRASSING"	"STRANGER"	"PRETTY ISN'T PRETTY"	"TEENAGE DREAM"	"SO AMERICAN"
"FAVORITE CRIME"	"BAD IDEA, RIGHT?"	"GIRL I'VE ALWAYS BEEN"	"JEALOUSY, JEALOUSY"	"BRUTAL"

TEAM ONE

"BALLAD OF A HOME-SCHOOLED G*RL"	"STRANGER"	"GET HIM BACK!"	"OBSESSED"	"VAMPIRE"
"SCARED OF MY GUITAR"	"1 STEP FORWARD, 3 STEPS BACK"	"TRAITOR"	"LACY"	"THE GRUDGE"
"GIRL I'VE ALWAYS BEEN"	"TEENAGE DREAM"	🧛	"ENOUGH FOR YOU"	"LOVE IS EMBAR-RASSING"
"MAKING THE BED"	"GOOD 4 U!"	"DRIVERS LICENSE"	"SO AMERICAN"	"BAD IDEA, RIGHT?"
"HOPE UR OK"	"LOGICAL"	"ALL-AMERICAN B*TCH"	"BRUTAL"	"DEJA VU"

TEAM TWO

BEHIND THE MUSIC CROSSWORD

Every superstar gets their inspiration from somewhere. Olivia credits these songs, musicians, and moments with giving her the guts to sing her heart out.

ACROSS

1. This iconic artist gave Olivia a book of poetry and inscribed "To Olivia, may all your days be inspired" on the inside pages.
4. Olivia said this Elizabeth Gilbert book is a "creative person's Bible" and is the only book she's ever read more than once.
5. She refers to this piano man in the song "deja vu."
7. Olivia credits author Julia Cameron's book with inspiring her handwritten, three-page writing ritual each morning.

DOWN

2. Olivia thinks this Adele song is the best piano ballad ever written.
3. She was thrifting with her mom when she bought her first album, named this, by Carol King.
6. This Fiona Apple song makes her cry.

BRUTAL BRACKET

Start your Olivia Rodrigo fantasy bracket! Compete with a friend by listing different Olivia Rodrigo songs in each of the far boxes. Shuffle your Olivia playlist until you get to one of the songs in the first bracket of competing boxes. Move that song to the next space and continue until you finish your Livie brackets.

BUTTERFLY OBSESSED QUIZ

Liv loves a butterfly. Take this quiz to see if you can spot the times Olivia has mentioned butterflies and their meaning, or used them as a fun visual in her style and videos.

1. Olivia wore these purple accessories in her hair at the 2022 Met Gala.

   _____

2. This song includes the lyric "holes in my butterfly wings" to express painful memories that can't be taken back.

   _____

3. In an interview, Olivia spoke about the growth of becoming an adult, highlighting that butterflies signify what in life?

   _____

4. Olivia has butterfly merch on her website, including a pool floatie, silver belt, silver ring, t-shirt, and this.

   _____

IN A COLLAB WORD SEARCH

Olivia got her start writing music while she was in the *High School Musical* series. She penned "All I Want" and cowrote "Just for a Moment" with her then costar and boyfriend Joshua Bassett. Check out Olivia's musical collaborators and see if you can find them in the word search.

```
S M A R B A E I C A R G D J
M O D B Z N D K Y V J D O L
A T R D R J V Z T S W S M D
D Q M G R M B B O M H R N X
I T Q Q I K X F Q U R R K Q
S T Q D Z N I Z A D E V M N
O R Y Z T A L B D D L B Z L
N L W Z W B A E N L R X V B
H L X Y L S L A I T M L N K
U X L Y S Y X X R N T Q L B
J I P E X E N T X P A N M K
E K T L L X K R J M G D W M
Q T V A N Q Y L Q V L M Y M
```

JOSHUA BASSETT
DANIEL NIGRO
GRACIE ABRAMS

MADISON HU
ALEXANDER 23
SOFIA WYLIE

THIS OR THAT

Sometimes you just have to choose. Find out which songs really matter to you by comparing two songs and circling your favorite.

"VAMPIRE"	OR	"BRUTAL"
"MAKING THE BED"	OR	"LACY"
"DRIVERS LICENSE"	OR	"GOOD 4 U"
"HOPE UR OK"	OR	"PRETTY ISN'T PRETTY"
"TEENAGE DREAM"	OR	"OBSESSED"
"SO AMERICAN"	OR	"GIRL I'VE ALWAYS BEEN"
"LOVE IS EMBARRASSING"	OR	"DEJA VU"
"TRAITOR"	OR	"FAVORITE CRIME"
"1 STEP FORWARD, 3 STEPS BACK"	OR	"LOGICAL"
"ENOUGH FOR YOU"	OR	"ALL-AMERICAN B*TCH"
"BAD IDEA RIGHT?"	OR	"GET HIM BACK!"
"BALLAD OF A HOMESCHOOLED GIRL"	OR	"THE GRUDGE"
"STRANGER"	OR	"SCARED OF MY GUITAR"
"JEALOUSY, JEALOUSY"	OR	"HAPPIER"

TRUE OR FALSE

Olivia is all about authenticity.
Can you tell what's real?

1. Olivia was once held at the Canadian-American border because US border agents mistook her for a person-of-interest named "Olivia Rodriguez."

   TRUE OR FALSE

2. "drivers license" refers to a blonde girl, but the original lyric referred to a redhead.

   TRUE OR FALSE

3. The "obsessed" music video was supposed to have a "hoodie return" at the debutante ball instead of a coat check.

   TRUE OR FALSE

4. Olivia's one regret about not having a normal teenage experience is that she never got to work as a lifeguard.

   TRUE OR FALSE

5. When Olivia visited the White House in 2021, President Biden gave her a bag of gifts that included a shoehorn.

   TRUE OR FALSE

LITTLE-KNOWN LIV CROSSWORD

Olivia has mastered the craft of being a medley of contradictions that somehow go together. Do you know some of these fun facts about her?

ACROSS

5   Olivia was "Team Edward" and had a poster of this movie on her wall as a kid.
6   Olivia purchased a purse by this luxury brand to reward herself for finishing SOUR.
7   Olivia first auditioned for this show when she was six and didn't get the part.
8   Her preferred way to shop.

DOWN

1   Her favorite McDonald's order.
2   She likes to go here with her parents on Christmas day.
3   Olivia bought a red plaid dress from Chlöe Sevigny that she'd been admiring on this social platform for years.
4   "And what it all comes down to / Is that everything's gonna be fine, fine, fine," is the lyric by this artist that Olivia lives by.

SONGS OF A *SOUR* SENSATION

Not all artists can produce banger after banger. Olivia's secrets to success are in her vulnerability, her willingness to experiment, and her playfulness. Below, you can find anagrams of some of her song titles. Use the clues to help you unscramble these hits.

1. This song is about Olivia accepting responsibility. The title plays on a popular axiom that ends with, "now lie in it."

   NGKMIA HTE DBE

   _____

2. The title of this song comes from Olivia's feelings of vulnerability when she plays music, with her instrument forcing her to be emotionally honest.

   CDSARE FO YM RGAITU

   _____

3. Many fans speculate that this song is about Olivia's ex and former costar of *High School Musical: The Musical*, Joshua Bassett.

   TITRRAO

   _____

4. This song off *SOUR* features the soft sounds of a hand-picked guitar.

   OARIVETF EMRCI

   _____

5. This song includes an incorrect math equation to express the burden of feeling foolish in an unbalanced romance.

   GLOILCA

   _____

6. This song includes a section with muffled voices that have been buried beneath layers of music. Here, her producer is actually saying, "What should the next four-letter album title be? Fart?"

GENTEAE ADREM

_____

7. This song is widely considered to be Olivia's first "love song" in her discography.

OS AMICNARE

_____

8. This upbeat song expresses the relief of waking up and realizing that you've gotten over an ex who once occupied most of your thoughts.

GNAERRTS

_____

9. Olivia used this song to express her frustration and the feelings of envy and comparison she felt while spending too much time on social media.

AUELOJSY, YEUOJSLA

_____

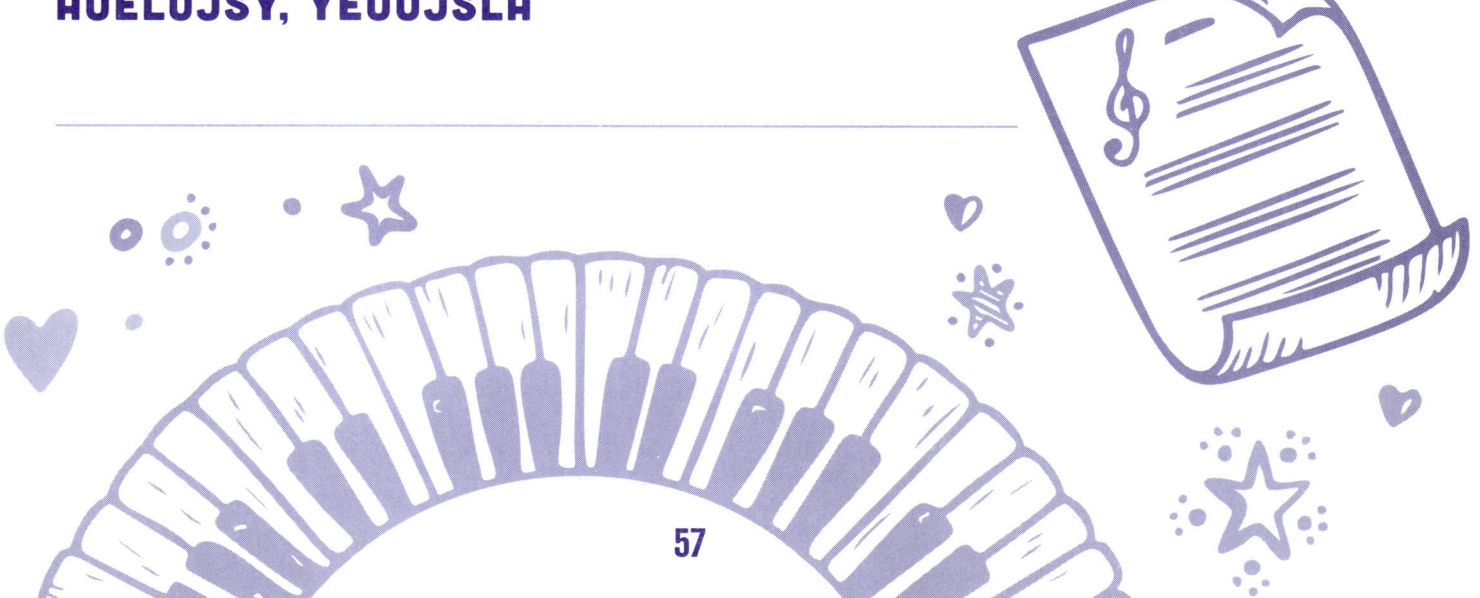

A SONGWRITER AT HEART

Songwriting doesn't happen on its own. As Olivia will tell you, she's written hundreds of songs and only a handful of them have made it to her records: "I've written so many bad songs in my life, and that's how you get to the good ones." She said there are specific components to good songwriting:

> 1. A GOOD TITLE AND GOOD CONCEPT
> 2. A MELODY THAT MOVES YOU
> 3. BELIEVE IN YOURSELF AND KEEP TRYING

Olivia says that her two favorite things a song can have are specificity and authenticity. And often, those two go hand in hand. If you can stir up specific images that evoke a feeling or a moment in time, you are more likely to elicit a sincere emotion from the listener.

Use Olivia's songwriting advice to create your own ballad. Whether you've had experience writing songs and poems or you prefer to journal, there's no better time to start than right now.

THE OLIVIA AESTHETIC WORD SEARCH

Olivia's album art is equal parts fun and ferocious, both peppy and totally unhinged. With stickers, sour candy, and tongues splashed across *SOUR* memorabilia and vampire teeth, sparkles, and puking jokes surrounding the *GUTS* album, her aesthetic makes her seem like someone you could totally hang out with. Find these Olivia-esque motifs in the word search.

```
V M A G A Z I N E S P K
A N S B B B V M V Q M S
M M B R Q S X Z W N E J
P M E G E N E D W I L L
I T S G Z K D I L X O X
R O T W A Z C F L L Y L
E N R S B P R I L I B J
T G A X T E H Y T W M Z
E U E R T A P O Y S J S
E E H T V O R R N N M P
T S U V P L J S B E M R
H B X Z P D Y M B N V B
```

HEARTS
STICKERS
SMILIES
VAMPIRE TEETH
TONGUES

MEGAPHONE
BUTTERFLIES
STARS
MAGAZINES
LOLLYPOP

OLIVIA'S ACCOLADES

When "drivers license" debuted and skyrocketed to the top of the charts, it also launched Olivia into a newfound superstardom. She recalls, "My entire life just, like, shifted in an instant." While albums like GUTS explore the complex feelings that come along with fame, Olivia's songwriting, outspokenness, and charm make her both relatable and extraordinary. It's no wonder she's been collecting awards and recognition ever since. In the empty spaces, write out what you admire about your favorite icon.

GRAMMY — BEST POP SOLO PERFORMANCE — "drivers license" — 2022 —

BILLBOARD — WOMAN OF THE YEAR — 2022 —

GRAMMY — BEST NEW ARTIST — SOUR — 2022 —

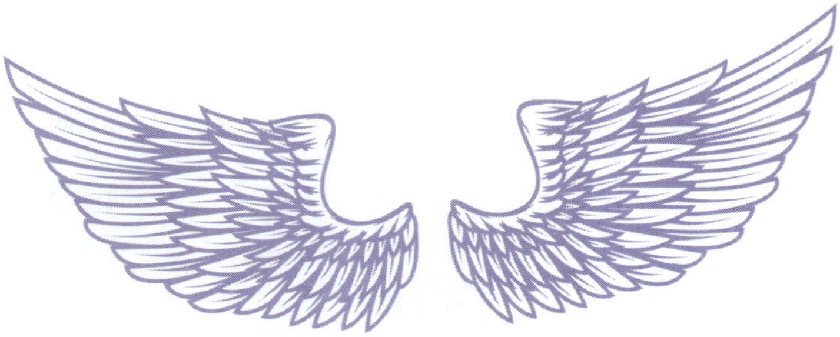

GIRL SHE'S ALWAYS BEEN CROSSWORD

Olivia has catapulted to fame in just a few short years. Along with hit records and brand endorsements, Olivia is friendly to her fans and reads like an open book to her interviewers. See if you've heard these fun facts about Liv.

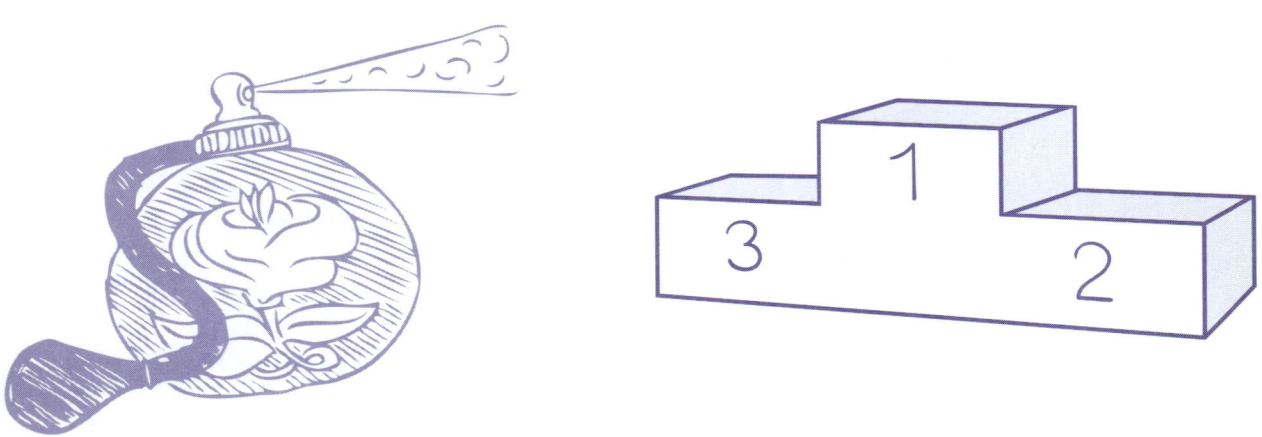

ACROSS
4 Olivia thinks she's best at this instrument.
5 Her album *GUTS* has its own dessert, this treat with a star cutout in the center.
6 She's the ambassador for this brand's Idôle Power perfume.
7 A simple pleasure she can't live without.

DOWN
1 Olivia eats this kind of sandwich before every show.
2 Olivia is very good at this elegant sport.
3 Her second live performance ever was on this popular show.
4 Olivia said angels would probably use Maison Francis Kurkdjian Baccarat Rouge 540, her favorite scent of this.

LIVIE BINGO

Turn up your Olivia radio and play bingo in teams of two. To make yourself a true Livie, put pieces of candy or stickers on the spaces that correspond to something you've done. Winner gets a glitter party.

YOU OWN *GUTS* ON VINYL	YOU STICK YOUR TONGUE OUT WHENEVER POSSIBLE	YOU'VE EATEN HER CRUMBL *GUTS* COOKIE	YOU APPLY HER BREAK-UP SONGS TO YOUR OWN LIFE	YOU'VE WORN BLACK NAIL POLISH
OLIVIA IS IN YOUR SPOTIFY WRAPPED	YOU MAKE OLIVIA FAN ART	YOU EAT STRAWBERRY ICE CREAM BECAUSE OF "DEJA VU"	YOU'VE DRESSED UP LIKE LIV FOR HALLOWEEN	VAMPIRE TEETH ARE YOUR AESTHETIC
YOU'RE AN ONLY CHILD	YOU'VE PERFECTED WINGED EYELINER	💋	YOU HAVE HER TOUR MERCH	YOU'VE SEEN *HIGH SCHOOL MUSICAL: THE MUSICAL: THE SERIES*
YOU OWN A STANLEY	YOU LIKE THRIFTING	YOU'VE PLAYED HER SONGS ON GUITAR	YOU CAN'T PARALLEL PARK	YOU'VE EMBRACED '90S FASHION
YOU FOLLOW LIV ON SOCIALS	YOU DECORATE WITH STICKERS	YOU SAW HER *GUTS* WORLD TOUR	YOU LISTEN TO "DRIVERS LICENSE" IN THE CAR	YOU HAVE AN OLIVIA TATTOO

TEAM ONE

66

YOU'VE EMBRACED '90S FASHION	YOU'VE SEEN *DRIVING HOME 2 U*	YOU'VE DRESSED UP LIKE LIV FOR HALLOWEEN	YOU OWN *SOUR* ON VINYL	YOU'VE PERFECTED WINGED EYELINER
YOU'VE EATEN HER CRUMBL *GUTS* COOKIE	YOU'VE PLAYED HER SONGS ON PIANO	YOU'VE PUT STICKERS ON YOUR FACE	YOU SAW HER *SOUR* WORLD TOUR	YOU'VE CRIED AT HER SONGS
YOU'VE SEEN *BIZAARDVARK*	BUTTERFLIES ARE YOUR AESTHETIC		YOU OWN A STANLEY	YOU CAN PARALLEL PARK
YOU WEAR PLAID	YOU HAVE AN OLIVIA TATTOO	YOU WRITE SONGS ABOUT YOUR FEELINGS	YOU LOVE SOUR CANDY	YOU'VE MADE OLIVIA FAN ART
YOU WANT TO JOIN AN ALL-GIRL BAND	YOU LISTEN TO BILLY JOEL BECAUSE OF HER	YOU NOW KNOW WHAT SYNESTHESIA IS	YOU APPLY HER SONGS TO YOUR OWN LIFE	PURPLE IS YOUR FAVORITE COLOR

TEAM TWO

CAUSES TO CARE ABOUT WORD SEARCH

Olivia is not shy in her beliefs, and she has always stood tall for the people she cares about. From writing compassionate lyrics in support of those growing up in unsafe circumstances ("hope ur ok") to building her own charitable foundations (Good 4 U Foundation), Liv knows how to show up. Find the key phrases in the word search.

Olivia is an active supporter of the epidermolysis bullosa (EB) community. Her efforts have led to millions of dollars in donations to fund research and help people with the disease. Those affected by EB are often called "butterfly children" because the condition makes their skin as delicate as a butterfly's wings. This gives Olivia's use of butterflies in her album aesthetics a whole new layer of meaning.

```
E C N E L O I V C I T S E M O D
Y T I L A U Q E R E D N E G P L
S T S P E Y S J D W R H N L T B
E S L E N D Q H B W T D G K N Q
R G E L S D U T E L J B K J Q Q
I N R N M A Q C A L T G M T M N
F I Q Z S B E E A Q T T D Q K J
D T L G R S H S R T Q E V L Q Y
L O N J J S E I I Z I Y R L W Q
I V L N N Q G L Z D T O N S T M
W L D E L H R R E R E W N D N R
J M M Q T J B P P M D R P T Z D
L O Z S D T N D X M O K A K T B
W D W G N Q R Z N Z B H K R Q Q
```

LGBTQ+ RIGHTS
EDUCATION
GENDER EQUALITY
SHELTERS
DOMESTIC VIOLENCE

HOMELESSNESS
VOTING
WILDFIRES
WOMEN'S HEALTH
RARE DISEASES

GET HIM BACK!

The song "get him back!" on *GUTS* is full of wordplay, using the phrase to mean two things. As Olivia sings it, she dreams of getting back together with her ex, while also working through a revenge fantasy of how to enact a little karma for his bad behavior. Use the space below to sort through which of Olivia's songs and lyrics make you feel good about love and which ones help you process your feelings about the tougher moments.

VAMPIRE BEHAVIOR

SONG: _____ ALBUM: _____
LYRICS: _____
_____
_____
_____

SONG: _____ ALBUM: _____
LYRICS: _____
_____
_____
_____

SONG: _____ ALBUM: _____
LYRICS: _____
_____
_____
_____

SONG: _____ ALBUM: _____
LYRICS: _____
_____
_____
_____

FEELING SOUR

SONG: _____ ALBUM: _____
LYRICS: _____
_____
_____
_____

SONG: _____ ALBUM: _____
LYRICS: _____
_____
_____
_____

SONG: _____ ALBUM: _____
LYRICS: _____
_____
_____
_____

SONG: _____ ALBUM: _____
LYRICS: _____
_____
_____
_____

ALL CONFIDENCE

SONG: _____ ALBUM: _____
LYRICS: _____
_____
_____
_____

SONG: _____ ALBUM: _____
LYRICS: _____
_____
_____
_____

SONG: _____ ALBUM: _____
LYRICS: _____
_____
_____
_____

SONG: _____ ALBUM: _____
LYRICS: _____
_____
_____
_____

SO MANY BUTTERFLIES

SONG: _____ ALBUM: _____
LYRICS: _____
_____
_____
_____

SONG: _____ ALBUM: _____
LYRICS: _____
_____
_____
_____

SONG: _____ ALBUM: _____
LYRICS: _____
_____
_____
_____

SONG: _____ ALBUM: _____
LYRICS: _____
_____
_____
_____

SONGS OF AN OLIVIA RODRIGO OBSESSIVE

A songwriter to her core, Olivia has a way with her pen that is clever and down-to-earth. She can write sweet or sour, and she stands out when she's willing to be messy and push the limit. The result? She's totally on point. Write out your favorite lyrics here.

CUTS DEEP

SONG: _____ ALBUM: _____
LYRICS: _____
_____
_____
_____

SONG: _____ ALBUM: _____
LYRICS: _____
_____
_____
_____

SONG: _____ ALBUM: _____
LYRICS: _____
_____
_____
_____

SONG: _____ ALBUM: _____
LYRICS: _____
_____
_____
_____

THIS GETS ME

SONG: _____ ALBUM: _____
LYRICS: _____
_____
_____
_____

SONG: _____ ALBUM: _____
LYRICS: _____
_____
_____
_____

SONG: _____ ALBUM: _____
LYRICS: _____
_____
_____
_____

SONG: _____ ALBUM: _____
LYRICS: _____
_____
_____
_____

IN A MOOD

SONG: _____ ALBUM: _____
LYRICS: _____
_____
_____
_____

SONG: _____ ALBUM: _____
LYRICS: _____
_____
_____
_____

SONG: _____ ALBUM: _____
LYRICS: _____
_____
_____
_____

SONG: _____ ALBUM: _____
LYRICS: _____
_____
_____
_____

ON TOP OF THE WORLD

SONG: _____ ALBUM: _____
LYRICS: _____
_____
_____
_____

SONG: _____ ALBUM: _____
LYRICS: _____
_____
_____
_____

SONG: _____ ALBUM: _____
LYRICS: _____
_____
_____
_____

SONG: _____ ALBUM: _____
LYRICS: _____
_____
_____
_____

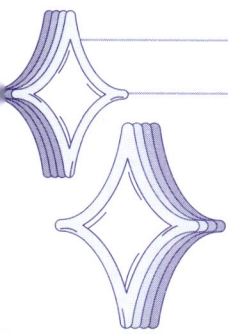

SOLUTIONS

PAGES 8-9
BALLADS OF AN ALL-AMERICAN SONGWRITER

1. "lacy"
2. "good 4 u"
3. "Can't Catch Me Now"
4. "all-american b*tch"
5. "drivers license"
6. "1 step forward, 3 steps back"
7. "vampire"
8. "bad idea, right?"
9. "get him back!"
10. "hope ur ok"

PAGES 10-11
INFLUENCING A SUPERSTAR WORD SEARCH

PAGES 16-17
ALL ABOUT OLIVIA CROSSWORD

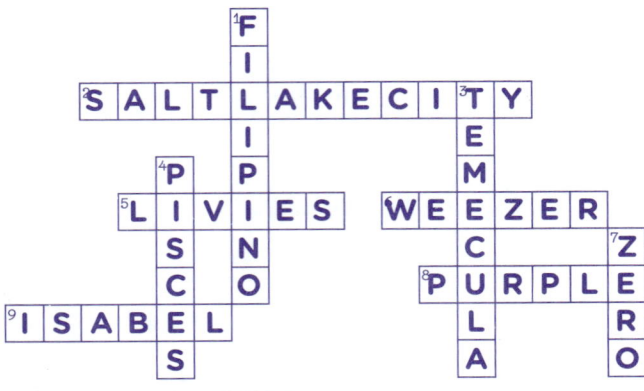

PAGES 18-19
GUITAR HEROINE QUIZ

1. *Bizaardvark*
2. "hope ur ok," "the grudge," and "lacy"
3. "obsessed"
4. Purple

PAGES 20-21
LIV'S LEAKED SONGS WORD SEARCH

```
S B T E A S T R O N A U T M D
E T D I V G T D Y S A T N A F
Z F R J U O V X X D L J R K S
T X I A M Q L K G B J W T O W
M Z X L N R I I N B R D B J Y
Q G R N R G E M S J D E V D W
J T M Y B O E T O E R Y S J M
B N B G R G F R T M N T N N L
Y T B D R R Q N S E R O W R W
T V G R P Y Q P O A B J E J K
N Y L M J R J T N S G O L H J
N M R Z D L N G B G I A D N T
J M T Z P R E R B B L R I T M
T L G J X M R M M D N V P N N
```

PAGES 24-25
LIVIE'S RAD SOUNDS CROSSWORD

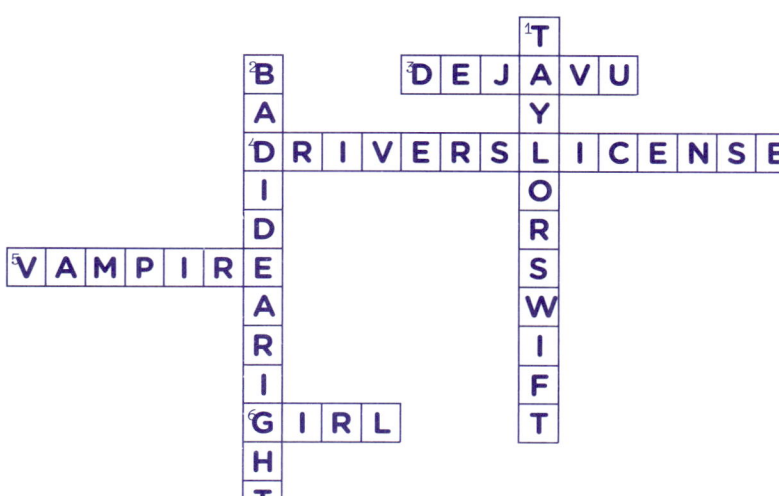

PAGES 26-27
RODRIGO RHYTHMS

1. "brutal"
2. "enough for you"
3. "obsessed"
4. "happier"
5. "deja vu"
6. "ballad of a homeschooled girl"
7. "the grudge"
8. "love is embarrassing"
9. "pretty isn't pretty"
10. "girl i've always been"

PAGES 30-31
THE BFFS WORD SEARCH

PAGES 34-35
OLIVIA'S FAVORITE THINGS CROSSWORD

76

PAGES 38-39
WILD FACTS QUIZ

1. "hope ur ok"
2. See color
3. Chappell Roan
4. *Twilight*

PAGES 40-41
LIV'S ICONIC FASHION WORD SEARCH

```
P Y T T Z L R J T P E Q Z V X
D A L Q J B X N Q N C Y P M Q
P R T L D N Q R X J A G P Q R
O K S T O O B K C A L B P Y X
L L D R D E T R I K S I N I M K
K G R M A R Y J A N E S P N J
A S M A P J N Z N Z V Y U B J
D Y N G P X Q E X W B P D L R
O T Y E X O N W D W B T B E J
T V L Z A D E G R T L B D N Z
J K Z P G K B L V T I L M V Q
D Y R G M Q E Z D L I G D L Q
J T W N B G Y R K P W K H K L
Q N N L J L D R S Y R X Y T J
X Y B Q L X J Y T P Y L N N S
```

PAGES 44-45
BEHIND THE MUSIC CROSSWORD

PAGES 48-49
BUTTERFLY OBSESSED QUIZ

1. Butterfly clips
2. "hope ur ok"
3. Transformation
4. Tote bag

PAGES 50-51
IN A COLLAB WORD SEARCH

```
S M A R B A E I C A R G D J
M O D B Z N D K Y V J D O L
A T R D R J V Z T S W S M D
D Q M G R M B B O M H R N X
I T Q Q I K X F Q U R R K Q
S T Q D Z N I Z A D E V M N
O R Y Z T A L B D D L B Z L
N L W Z W B A E N L R X V B
H L X Y L S L A I T M L N K
U X L Y S Y X X R N T Q L B
J I P E X E N T X P A N M K
E K T L L X K R J M G D W M
Q T V A N Q Y L Q V L M Y M
```

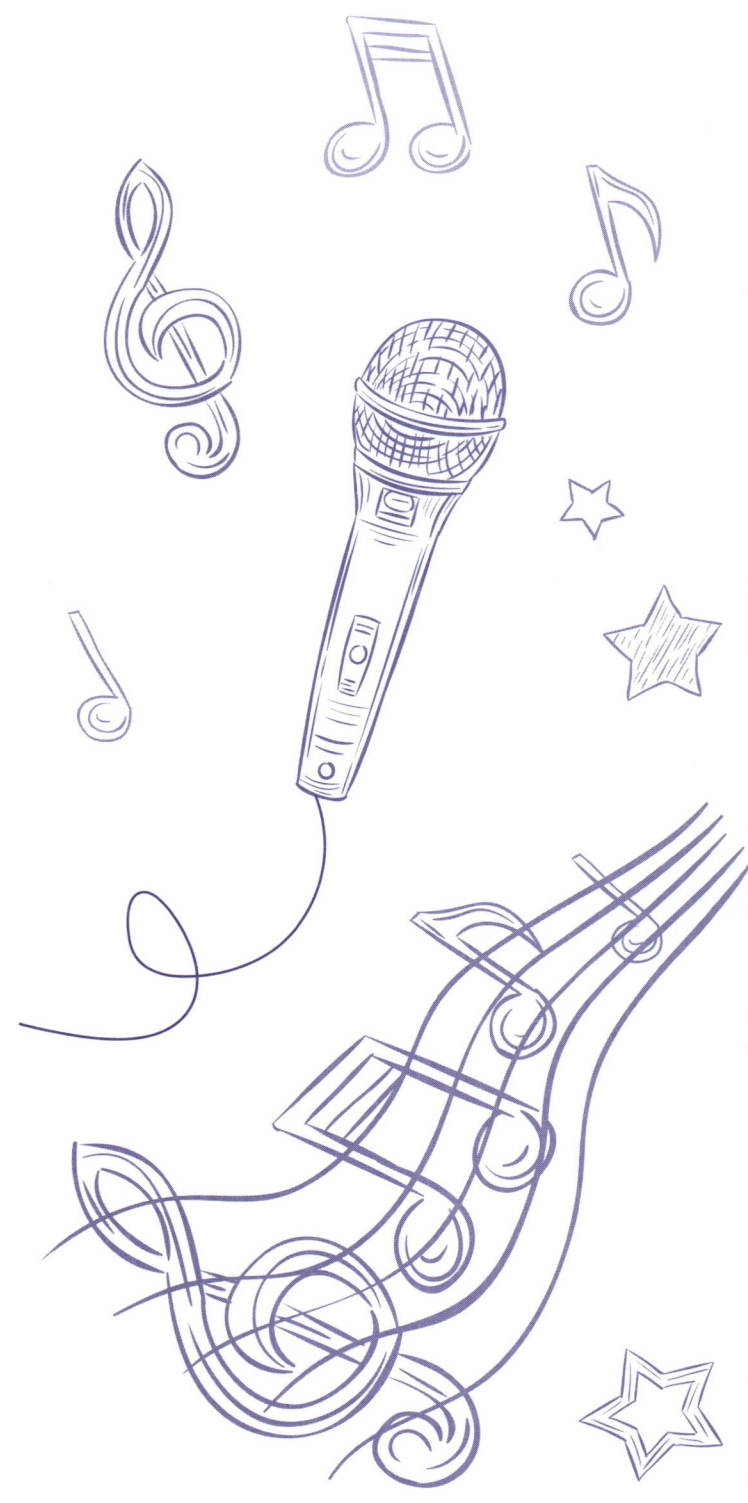

PAGE 53
TRUE OR FALSE

1. **True.** They held her for questioning for thirty minutes until they realized they had the wrong person.
2. **False.** The original lyric in her first online post of the song was "brunette."
3. **True.** The scene was cut from the final music video, but it was part of an extensive set design.
4. **False.** She wishes she could have been a babysitter.
5. **False.** Olivia thought it was a shoehorn, but it was actually a presidential ice cream scoop.

PAGES 54-55
LITTLE-KNOWN LIV CROSSWORD

PAGES 56-57
SONGS OF A *SOUR* SENSATION

1. "making the bed"
2. "scared of my guitar"
3. "traitor"
4. "favorite crime"
5. "logical"
6. "teenage dream"
7. "so american"
8. "stranger"
9. "jealousy, jealousy"

PAGES 60-61
THE OLIVIA AESTHETIC WORD SEARCH

PAGES 64-65
GIRL SHE'S ALWAYS BEEN CROSSWORD

PAGES 68-69
CAUSES TO CARE ABOUT WORD SEARCH

ABOUT THE AUTHOR

Lucy Ledesma is a pop culture writer. When she isn't tracing celebrity timelines, you can find her outside listening to old cassettes on her 1990s Walkman. She lives in San Clemente, California with her family.